30 days to a Biblical Worldview

A Great Christian Book

30 days to a Biblical Worldview

Chris Hatton

A GREAT CHRISTIAN BOOKS publication
Great Christian Books is a division of Rotolo Media
160 37th Street Lindenhurst, New York 11757
(631) 956-0998
www.GreatChristianBooks.com
email: mail@greatchristianbooks.com

Hatton, Chris, 1970-
    30 days to a biblical worldview / by Chris Hatton
        p.   cm.
A "A Great Christian Book" book
GREAT CHRISTIAN BOOKS a division of Rotolo Media
ISBN 0-9670840-6-7
Recommended Dewey Decimal Classifications: 204, 230, 234
Suggested Subject Headings:
1. Religion—Christian literature—Worldview
2. Christianity—The Bible—Practical Theology
I. Title

*The book and cover design for this title are by Michael Rotolo.
It is typeset in the Minion and Myriad typefaces by Adobe Inc. and is quality manufactured in the United States on premium, archival quality acid-free paper stock.*

To discuss the publication of your Christian manuscript or out-of-print book , please contact Great Christian Books.

MANUFACTURED IN THE GREAT UNITED STATES OF AMERICA

"Pastor Chris Hatton has compiled a selection of current topics and issues and has brought Biblical principles to bear upon the various problems, difficulties and dilemmas confronting contemporary society. Within the compass of this small volume, a range of subjects are covered including the basic fundamental need of man to be reconciled to his Maker. The closing chapter reminds us of the absolutely certain fact, whether a person believes it or not, that a great day of accountability looms before every single mortal who has ever drawn breath! I would heartily recommend this little book and the succinct manner in which it addresses such serious issues."

—Jim Handyside

Pastor of the Reformed Baptist Church in Glasgow, Scotland
Author of *Portrait of a Master Craftsman* and *Melt the Icebergs!*

"It is a delight for me to recommend this little volume you are holding in your hands. Pastor Chris Hatton is not only a dear brother in Christ, co-laborer in the ministry and friend— he is a man with a Pastor's heart. His love for God, His people and the preaching of the Word is evident to all those who have had the privilege of serving with him. Chris takes seriously the call to be an overseer of those entrusted to his care and does so with compassion and determination. In this book you will find the heart of a shepherd as he reveals his concern for the spiritual welfare of God's people. You will also find on the following pages the author's answers to many issues facing today's Church. It is my prayer and I'm sure Chris' prayer as well that this book will first and foremost bring glory to God and be used by Him in the lives of His people in a very special and unique way."

—Hugh R. Diggins Sr.

Pastor of Reformed Bible Church of Pittsford, Vermont

Contents

Day1

A TERMINAL ILLNESS

"Wherefore, as by one man sin entered into the
world, and death by sin; and so death passed upon
all men, for that all have sinned." —Romans 5:12

It is sad how we have undermined the universal problem of all mankind. We too often overlook the problem
as we treat the symptoms. When was the last time that
you read an obituary or a death certificate that stated the
cause of death as "Sin"? The reason why we die is not cancer, diabetes, or even old age. Man's rebellion against his
Creator has caused this tragic reality.

Before sin came into the world, death did not exist.
You may recall the gracious warning that God gave to
our federal head in the garden. Adam was told not to eat,
lest he surely die. This death was both immediate and
progressive. Although the Lord had created man good,
pure, and morally upright, sin corrupted that nature and
condition. There was an immediate death within the

heart of man. His moral ability to live in fellowship with his holy Creator was Lost with a capitol L. He became spiritually bankrupt and now stood before God naked and ashamed.

Ever since sin entered the heart of mankind in Adam he has been hiding from the presence of God. This does not mean that man cannot do *anything* good. It means that all of man's good is not pleasing to God unless the rebellious nature has first been dealt with. No amount of good deeds can earn an overlooking of man's sin. There must be a sincere repentance and faith in the redemptive work of God's Son. This sin problem also began a process of slow physical death. We call it growing or aging. We have made it as nice as we can by focusing on some "positive" aspects of this process of slow, physical death.

We speak in terms of euphemisms like "stronger", "bigger", and hopefully "wiser". We try to minimize how awful this process makes us look. From make-up to nip and tucks, we seek to halt this aging process and stay as young looking as we can. Even with an extreme makeover, our body relentlessly continues its countdown to decay. The reality is that we are all terminally ill with a disease called Sin. It is a universal problem and is the cause of death for all of us. Some may choose denial, but death still comes. This problem is not the fault of God. He made us good, but we chose to rebel against His word. Understanding our illness should be our goal once we accept the diagnosis.

The "good news" is that God has given us a cure and tells us exactly how to treat the problem and the symptoms. He is a Great Physician! He has sent His Son to shed His blood that we might have life. Our condition before God is remedied through faith in Christ. Regeneration brings reformation to our heart and life. Not only are we enabled to enjoy sweet fellowship with the Creator against whom we have rebelled, but we are also given principles and power to keep us from future sin as well. He is able to keep us from falling and has taken away the sting of death.

Though we may walk through the valley of death, we have the overwhelming presence of our Lord to comfort us. He will carry us safely to His heavenly kingdom and will one day cast sin and death into the abyss.

Day 2

A PLANNED PREGNANCY

"Blessed be the God and Father of our Lord Jesus
Christ, which according to His abundant mercy
hath begotten us again unto a lively hope by the
resurrection of Jesus Christ from the dead."
—1 Peter 1:3

Becoming a believer in Christ is meant to bring such a radical change that it is often described in the Bible as a new birth. Faith in Christ comes by hearing the word of God. Whether we read the Gospel, hear the Gospel, or see the Gospel lived out in the lives of those who have been changed by it, we cannot understand or comprehend the truth of it without the aid and work of God. As our paternal spiritual Father, He desires to cause our new birth and then initiates all that is needed to bring it to pass.

There are no Christian mistakes in the family of God. It makes our entrance grander to see that our faith was the direct result of what God both willed and worked out. I think the most often neglected and overlooked verse in the book of John is John 1:13, but it needs to be taken in context with verse twelve:

> *But as many as received Him, to them gave He power to become the sons of God, even to them that believe on His name; Which were born, not of blood, nor of the will of the flesh, nor of the will of man, but of God.*
> *—John 1:12-13*

The receiving of Christ and the adoption as a child of God constitutes a new birth that was not the result of the will of man, but of the direct and planned will of God. He chose to adopt us not because of any good work or emotional decision that we could make, but rather out of His pure love, mercy, and grace. In my early years as a believer, I did not understand this. I thought it was my intellect or good luck that enabled me to figure out this truth about Christ. I seriously misunderstood the depth of my depravity.

Sin has so corrupted man that he is unable to comprehend truth outside of the work of the Holy Spirit. Nonbelieving mankind will not desire the truth of the Word of God and view the preaching of the cross as foolishness. This inability is expressed elsewhere in the Scriptures with two rhetorical questions:

> *Can the Ethiopian change his skin, or the leopard his spots? Then may ye also do good, that are accustomed to do evil. —Jeremiah 13:23*

We are so used to doing evil (a refusal to submit to God's law), that it would take a miracle of amazing grace to make a sinner accustomed to doing what the Lord requires. This miracle is what God does to each of His children as He causes them to become anew in Christ and gives them the gift of faith. Once the Sovereignty of God is applied to our salvation, we take further steps in Christian humility and a deeper perception of the wonderful matchless grace of Jesus.

In His own time and with the use of various means, God Himself draws the sinner to Christ. He imparts a conviction of sin and a convincing of what is really the Truth. He gives us His Spirit, which enables us to cry out to Him for mercy and grace as our Abba (Father).

Day 3

THE BASIS OF MORAL ABSOLUTES

"Think not that I am come to destroy the law."
—Matthew 5:17

When a sinner becomes converted to Christ, there springs up within his soul a hunger and thirst for righteousness. He loves the Lord that bought him with His precious blood and desires to live a life that is pleasing to Him. He wants to do what is right and pleasing in the sight of his God. Is there a sense of right and wrong? If so, to where shall we go to get such instruction in holy living?

It is true that all of mankind have innately within them a sense of moral right and wrong. Though suppressed by seared consciences, God has written His law within the heart of man. He has also written His Law on tablets of stone. The Ten Commandments were especially singled out from the many other of God's laws. When something is written in stone, it shows both authority and a timeless relevance. These out of all others were written by the very finger of God.

These Ten were supremely placed within the ark that contained the glory of God. These Ten are the foundation for all others. They are a basis for what is right and what is wrong. Love is the culmination for fulfilling the Law. If we love God, we will not violate the first four commands. If we love our neighbor, we will not violate the last six. When we violate any of the commands, it reveals a lack of love in our heart (our old nature). These are not ten suggestions or simple seeds for discussion and debate.

Indeed the Ten Commandments are a basis for moral absolutes. Jesus did not come to destroy the Law, and it is contrary to our text above to think in this way. He fulfilled all righteousness by His complete obedience to the Law. The Law was his standard for right and wrong and so it is for us. Though there were civil or judicial laws given to the theocratic nation of Israel, the Lord has instituted other national governments and has commanded His people to obey such powers that be (so long as the civil law does not violate any of the Higher Law of God).

There were also ceremonial Laws that were given as types and shadows of the coming Messiah. These are no longer necessary, as in Christ, we have the reality which they prefigured. So the Law is not destroyed, abolished, or rendered irrelevant, for the Christian. It remains as a standard for righteousness and holy living that pleases God. As such it will show man his sin and need for the mediatorial work of Christ.

Wherefore the law was our schoolmaster to bring us unto Christ, that we might be justified by faith.
—*Galatians 3:24*

The Law is a great evangelistic tool. The Ten Commandments of Exodus 20 is the "Romans Road"[1] of the Old Testament. Not only is it meant to be used evangelistically, but also for growth in holiness. When the Law is exposited, sinners are made aware of their need for Christ, and Saints are kept on a path of sanctification.

The Law will teach us to daily depend upon Christ and His ever enduring mercy as it unfolds more and more of our sinful hearts.

---

1   The Romans Road is the name given to a group of Bible verses from the Book of Romans that has been used as a quick consideration of the major points of the Gospel. These verses typically include most of the following verses: Romans 1:20-21, 3:23, 5:1, 5:8, 6:23a, 6:23b, 8:1, 8:38-39, 10:9-10, 10:13, and 11:36.

Day 4

THE DELIGHT OF THE LORD'S DAY

"The sabbath was made for man." —Mark 2:27

The Lord desired His people to remember the Sabbath principle and to keep the designing purpose of it in a holy way. This was not intended to be a burdensome religious duty that benefited God to see man suffer. God made the Sabbath Day principle for the benefit of mankind. Though the New Testament terms this the Lord's Day, the principle remains the same. The New Covenant believers observed one day out of seven as a special day to worship Christ and fellowship with one another.

This day was the time for them to give themselves to breaking bread together, praying with and for one another, and the study of Apostolic Doctrine. Thus we have the Sabbath principle brought forth and lived out in the New Covenant. It was never intended to be a strict legalistic list of do's and don'ts. When God rested on the seventh day of creation, it was not because he was physically tired or spiritually exhausted. He was setting a standard for the busy laborious work week of man. It was His divine blue law whereby man would receive a much needed benefit by observing. Man was not made for the purpose of becoming a slave or worshipper of the Sabbath. The Sabbath was made by God to bring refreshment and much needed strength and encouragement to man in the midst of each arduous week.

The Lord's people left their first love for God, though, and in turn did not delight in the Lord's Day. Their hearts became dull and, consequently, their view of the Lord's Day worship and the exercise of spiritual disciplines became dull. This is why the Lord moved Isaiah to write:

> *"If thou turn away thy foot from the sabbath, from doing thy pleasure on my holy day; and call the sabbath a delight, the holy of the LORD, honourable; and shalt honour him, not doing thine own ways, nor finding thine own pleasure, nor speaking thine own words: Then shalt thou delight thyself in the LORD; and I will cause thee to ride upon the high places of the earth, and feed thee with the heritage of Jacob thy father." —Isaiah 58:13-14*

They lost delight for the Lord and therefore had no delight in the one day of seven that was set aside to gather together for corporate worship. What a joy it is that the saint has a family to go to for encouragement. What a privilege it is to hear the Gospel proclaimed with authority and spiritual unction! What a blessing it is to see sinners enter the waters of Baptism! What comfort and grace comes to the believer as we partake of the Lord's Supper. Is it not exciting to experience the love of brethren whose hearts are knit together with like precious faith?

Should we wonder why David would say:

> *"For a day in thy courts is better than a thousand. I had rather be a doorkeeper in the house of my God, than to dwell in the tents of wickedness." —Psalm 84:10*

Ah, to hear the redeemed sing praises to Jesus! To see children being brought to the feet of Christ as two or more of His elect are gathered in His name. All this excitment happens on the Lord's Day when His people gather together. We are told not to forsake these gatherings because they are for our benefit. However many spots the church may have, it is a delight to be amidst the bride of Christ as she gathers.

Day 5

BROKEN CHINA

"Unto the woman He said, I will greatly multiply thy
sorrow and thy conception; in sorrow thou shalt
bring forth children; and thy desire shall be to thy
husband, and he shall rule over thee."
—Genesis 3:16

What a glorious day of surgery it was when God took
a rib from man and made woman. Oh, the pleasant surprise it must have been for Adam to behold the beauty
of Eve. God Himself walked her down the aisle and gave
her away to the man in holy matrimony. It was not good
for man to be alone and now he had the helper that he
needed. There, in the very beginning, we have record of
the role and purpose of the creation of woman.

The two were of one mind and walked in complete
harmony as husband and wife. Both understood their
God-given role and thus functioned peacefully and happily. Although their roles were different, they were both

absolutely equal in worth and value in the sight of God. Then came the fall, and sin ruined it all. Many are familiar with the consequences given. The Serpent would be on his belly with every intention of everlasting enmity toward the Seed of the woman. Man would die to return to the dust of the ground from which he was taken. Only by the sweat of our brow would we eat. The woman was given pain in child-bearing and something else...

She was also told that she would bear the curse of an innate desire to rule over the man. Sin has so tainted her heart that she will no longer desire to submit to her God given purpose and role at creation. She was to be a submissive helper to her husband, but would now desire to usurp man's authority and rule over him. A power struggle would now commence in the home, the workplace, and in the church! All of the tension that ensues can be traced to this sinful desire in the heart of the woman to rule over the man.

It is true that many women are better than some men in many ways. Women can be stronger than some men. Women can be wiser than some men. Women can be better providers than some men. But we need to understand that the God ordained role and function of a woman is not based upon her having inferior abilities. The woman is equal in worth, value, and dignity in God's sight, and can be better functioning than a man in many respects.

The question is not who is better at what, but rather what was God's design and purpose for the role of a woman and how has sin affected that Divine purpose? The Biblical mandate for the woman to be submissive does not make her a doormat to be walked on and abused. Any wise man will recognize that his wife is a gracious gift from God and that she has been given to him to help him in all that he does. The wife will have much needed insight and counsel for the man as he makes his decisions. While her primary role involves keeping the house and training their children, she remains a strong asset in many other ways. She has liberty to utilize her talents and abilities so long as she does so in submission to her husband and without usurping his authority.

Where there is an understanding of these roles and a heart to carry them out, there will be peace and happiness. When they are neglected, and the woman succumbs to this sinful desire to rule, there will be utter chaos and tension in the home, workplace, and even in the church. Even though some men do not love their wives as they ought, the principle of submission still stands (so long as the husband does not ask his wife to violate the law of God). Children are left with unwanted and undue stress when Mom struggles to rule over Dad and his God given authority as head in the home.

Day 6

OPTIMISTIC ESCHATOLOGY

"I will build My church; and the gates of hell shall not prevail against it." — Matthew 16:18

The Christian life is one of constant battle. There are struggles from within our own flesh, struggles with the worldly culture around us, and from that old Lion, Satan, who is always roaming about seeking to devour. On top of our own struggle to stay along the straight and narrow path, we have sin affecting our families, our communities, and indeed the world. It seems as if at any given moment, we can tune in to live media with eyewitness accounts of wars and rumors of wars. Regardless of where we turn we can find tribulation as the Christian world view is challenged, threatened, and attacked.

While we may expect the world to only get worse as they remain outside of Christ, sometimes we are surprised to see Christians and churches overtaken in faults. There are "End Time" gurus constantly warning us about how bad things are getting and that it will only get worse. Some are crying that the church age is over, and that we ought to leave the organized church because it has been overcome by evil. This kind of bombardment may lead some to hoard canned goods, stockpile weaponry, and escape the world. Such spiritual depression makes you want to give up and cry out like Elijah, "I am the only one left!"

So what should be our take upon Terrorism and how is the inquiring mind to know whether Gog and Magog symbolize Iran, Russia, North Korea, or...? May I suggest that there is much hope in not only resting in the absolute Sovereign control of an omniscient and omnipotent God, but also upon the promise He makes in Matthew:

"I will build My church; and the gates of hell shall not prevail against it." — Matthew 16:18

This passage is a Romans 8:28 view for the future. All things will work themselves out for our benefit. We must see the book of history as already having been written. The Lord knows the end from the beginning. He ultimately controls all of history. Though there is a dark force of evil in the world, Christ is building His church in the midst of it all. It is a great comfort to know that He is actively, sovereignly, building His church. The salvation of souls is not dependant upon our business savvy to market the gospel. Although we are commanded to "go" and make disciples of all the nations it is Jesus Himself who will build His church in spite of our often too feeble efforts. He does this by opening hearts of sinners and adding them to the church. He uses believers as precious stones and adds them, one at a time, to the many other members of the universal church. He also strengthens the church by causing His saints to grow in grace.

It is interesting to note that trials are the means by which many sinners come to Christ, and they are also the usual means by which Christians turn more to Christ and thereby grow in grace! Many have tried to stomp out the church, but the church only spreads and increases. As Tertullian said, "The blood of the martyrs is the seed of the Church." Times even may go from bad to worse as the pendulum of ungodliness in the world swings to the left and the right, but Christ will not stop building His church! The church will be militant and continue to fight a good fight with a persevering spirit, especially in light of this hope!

Though pessimism breeds depression and inactivity, knowledge of the church triumphant will help us get through difficulties. No matter how bad things may get, Jesus will use us to further His church and His kingdom of grace will always advance and ultimately triumph over all evil!

Day 7

THE FRUIT OF HOLINESS

"Follow peace with all men, and holiness, without which no man shall see the Lord."
— Hebrews 12:14

Jesus has likened life as to a tree. It was His rational logic to say that a tree is known by its fruit. If you see a bunch of apples hanging from the limbs, you can be sure that it is an apple tree. Likewise, the Christian will evidence a sincere faith with certain fruit. Now, this fruit does not come before the tree. It is not as though we seek to behave or live a certain way to become a Christian. The seed of the gospel is planted in the heart, watered with prayer, and warmed by the Son until it sprouts.

This seed continues to be divinely taken care of by various means until it is brought to fruition. There are several types of fruit on the believers' tree. I simply would like to touch upon the one that is most often neglected— Holiness.

Holiness begins at salvation and progresses until glorification. The new birth begins a life-long pursuit of Holy living in the heart of each new believer. Holiness is a heart passion for righteous living in order to please the very heart of Christ. As a child longs to please his father, so does the Christian, compelled by a love for Christ to adorn himself with holiness.

Many have dismissed the pursuit of holiness because it is impossible to maintain the standard. It is natural to succumb to frustration from time to time when we fall short of the glory of God and our hearts become side-tracked from Him; but we must remember that holiness is not perfection. It is not so much *what* is done, but the *motivational factor* behind the good that is done. Holiness is making things right when we do wrong. Holiness is a constant humility born out of a true knowledge of our inadequacy coupled with a dependency upon Christ to give us grace to accomplish our tasks with a right spirit and to forgive us when we sin.

Christians are first and foremost sinners. By default, we look to Christ from whom is our help. Now this fruit is said to become better and sweeter as the years go by. There will be a growth in such grace. The branch will not bear perfect fruit, so it will be pruned and cut back. A pursuit of holiness is desired by the Christian because within the heart there is a hatred for sin as the cause of all of life's problems. The Spirit of Holiness is what takes up residency in each believer. The Holy Spirit becomes quenched and grieved when we sin, and His convicting work will make us miserable while we continue outside of fellowship with Him. This process will be in the life of every true Christian.

This serves as a good basis for self-examination. If this is not the experience of any person that professes Christ as their Savior, then an attachment to the Vine of Life that is the only source of such fruit, is lacking. It is far too easy to merely attend church, carry a Bible, and adhere to a set of religious standards. Satan is pleased with keeping and using these deceived ones, who strut about adorned with haloes of self-righteousness. It is not enough to do "good" works in the name of Jesus. Many on the last day will proudly step forth to take credit for such deeds, only to hear "Depart from me ye workers of iniquity." Only those who genuinely seek to live a life of holiness consecrated to God will hear "Well done, good and faithful servant..."

Day 8

SPIRITUAL SPANKING
IN THE AGE OF TIME-OUTS

"For whom the Lord loveth He chasteneth, and
scourgeth every son whom He receiveth."
—Hebrews 12:6

I can recall my training to become state certified in
Foster and Adoptive care. The state devoted an entire ses-
sion on discipline. Many of the children in this system
would need much love, but not at the expense of discipline. The instructor was very careful to begin by stating
"NO SPANKING".

He proceeded to encourage several alternatives because any type of spanking was considered abuse. Now,
we can be sure that child abuse is real and wrong. My
question to the instructor was why do away with one
means of discipline when all the others can become abusive also? How many hours in time-out does it take to
become abusive? Many in the class shared how they were

raised with spanking and grew up without negative consequences, even "pretty good" by their reckoning. It was as if they were glad that they had parents that spanked them. Some acknowledged that there were times when Mom or Dad's anger got the best of them, but overall they sensed parental love in their childhood chastening and were better off for it.

Our modern fear of damaging a child's self-esteem has challenged God's prescription for discipline. It's as if we can never say: "That was wrong!" To do so we're told could risk "scarring" our children mentally with the accusation of their having "sinned." Even many parents who call themselves Christian are averse to administering consequences to their children by the prescription of discipline laid out in Scripture. Though we are given the option to allow love to cover a multitude of sins, we are not to constantly sweep sin under the carpet, especially when it is habitual. It is the glory of a man to overlook a fault and not be easily offended, but a neglect of the rod will spoil the child.

The same principle though is true in the life of believers. Just as children desperately need corrective discipline, we also need God's chastening. It can be said that God "spanks" His children, but He never does so in a capricious or abusive manner. The chastening "rod" of the Lord is always used in love and with the distinct purpose of correction and restoration.

Though there is pain enough in losing our fellowship with Christ, the Lord uses additional means to chasten us. He can use sickness as he did to Jezebel, or the believers in Corinth as they partook of the Lord's Table in an unworthy manner. A minor cold may not be minor at all. The Lord may be pruning us and purging out remaining dross of sin in our hearts. He can stir up a tempest in the home. Peter warned husbands to dwell with their wives in a godly way lest their prayers become hindered. The Lord can use the workplace to add stress to His wayward child. The Lord can use Satan to destroy the flesh. The Lord can use physical calamity (i.e., "natural disasters", "acts of God") and He can bring financial ruin.

Though Job was a righteous man that experienced his share of trouble, his three friends did not believe God was above using them as a means to deal with sin. It has been my experience in the local church that the Lord can effectively use that institution to recapture wayward brethren. The "spanking" steps of church discipline are outlined in Matthew 18:15-17. The main hindrance to this means of restoration is the reluctance of folks in the church to embrace it as God's ordained method of restoration. It will be difficult, but when done in love for the right purpose, it can break down the wall of a hardened heart and bring back a wayward soul. One mark of a church of Christ is people that practice Biblical discipline.

Day 9

THE HOLY SPIRIT NEGLECTED

"If we live in the Spirit, let us also walk in the Spirit."
—Galatians 5:25

It was a sad day for me when I was requested to identify the body of my father at the morgue. There he lay dormant with eyes shut. It was a morbid and utterly depressing feeling. The body that I was attached to by birth did not exhibit the life that had once given me joy. I get a similar feeling in the midst of some churches and believers. I often observe the external, visible aspects of the body of Christ, but sense a lack of the abundant life and joy that Christ came to give. It is possible for Christians to live a good life "externally" while neglecting the "inward" work of the Holy Spirit that gave them new life in Christ. I am not speaking of one who does not have life, real eternal life. Yes, we can only have life by having the Spirit, but there is a complete and radical difference between having the Spirit and walking in the Spirit that we have. He is always working, but we can grieve and quench His work. He is the one that guides us into all Truth, but we can neglect His ministry and remain in need of spiritual meat for years. He is the one that convicts us of sin, but we can become dull to His ministry. He desires to fill our cups and have them continually running over with Love. We will love our family more. We will love our lost neighbors more. We will love the brethren more. This cannot happen without walking in the Spirit.

Walking in the Spirit is not the throwing away of common sense. It is not something that needs forty-five minutes of praise music to ignite. Nor is it something that we wait to be struck with when the wind blows at random. This walk is the way in which believers should seek to purposely live on a daily basis as they yield to the guidance of the Holy Spirit. Something is amiss if this heart love for Christ and others is lacking. Love is the greatest commandment, and it cannot be obeyed without the ministry of the Spirit of God. It requires sensitivity and yielding to He who resides within us. It is something for which we must constantly pray.

It often amazes me how we can be so energetic in our pursuit of orthodox truth, yet dead in our walk. Let me give you some signs of this walk. There will be a high esteem for Pastors who feed souls well. There will be a desire to use one's gifts to help advance the local church ministry. There will be a priority placed upon prayer. There will be mercy and compassion shown to the least of God's children. It is easy to greet the clean looking friendly face in the next pew, but what do we do when someone comes into the church that looks destitute or different? Can we get past the way they dress or even smell? What about when a new attendee comes into the church and we know that they are not seeking a morally pure life? Are we able to approach such a one in love and greet them with a holy kiss? Is there room in our church for one that is very different from us? Does our attitude reflect an open and kind embrace for other fellow sinners? Is there room in our hearts, our churches, and our homes, for the building of relationships with the unsaved? Will a new, weak or immature believer feel accepted or will they detect "vibes" coming from us that make them feel unwelcome?

I think the modern hip-hop lyricist said it well when he penned the southern phrase, "Where is the love y'all?"

Day 10

DIVINE INSTITUTIONS

"What therefore God hath joined together,
let not man put asunder." —Matthew 19:6

My wife and I both come from broken homes, due to a spirit of divorce. This spirit was a symptom of a deeper problem. According to the verse above, God was the one that divinely joined each of our moms and dads together in marriage. Perhaps if they understood the larger picture, they would have remained together.

God is the one that made the institution that we call the family. He created Eve and as a loving father "gave away the bride" in the first ever marriage ceremony, which he instituted. He gave Eve to Adam and Adam to Eve. He joined them together as one flesh. Though Moses allowed for divorce because of hardened hearts, from the beginning it was not so. Marriage is God's design, and our text shows us how the Lord providentially places each and every couple together. Many have been seeking to undermine this sacred institution. The breakdown of the family is the devil's tool to destroy the world. The origin of marriage is not an invention of Dr. Dobson. Though it is old, marriage is not archaic baggage that needs to be discarded. It has withstood the test of time and brought happiness and stability to countless generations.

The family is a covenant community that comes with responsibility. The children are responsible to honor their father and mother with heart and obedience. The parents are to provide, protect, pray for, and train up their children. Some do real well with providing, but severely neglect the other God-ordained responsibilities. Some give their children great secular educations, but fail to teach them about their responsibility to their Creator. Should we wonder why some children want nothing to do with Church or the Bible when their parents fail to stress the blessing of such? You understand that God also established the Church.

Marriage is a picture of the loving relationship that Christ has for His bride, the Church. He birthed her into existence and covenanted her hand in the holy matrimony of salvation. She has the heart of God in her and for her. He loved her so much that He gave His life for her. Have you ever heard someone talk about the church in a negative way? How do you suppose I would feel if you spoke badly about my wife? The church body is attached to her head. We cannot treat the church in a neglectful way without doing the same to Christ.

The Church and the Family are not optional or suggested institutions. God's desire is that each person be joined to a family, and He has joined each believer to the church. These are for our good. It is a great blessing to be part of a family. Sure, there are no perfect families on earth. Each has its own difficulties and obstacles to godliness. These are meant to help us and mold us further into the image of the Lord Jesus. Why allow the spirit of divorce to take our hearts away from our God-ordained families and churches? We cannot put aside these institutions without rebelling against the one that divinely instituted them. There are grievous consequences when we do.

The Lord has established the governing powers that be. Whether in the home, society, the workplace, or the church, we need to have a proper respect and honor for what God hath joined us to. While we may expect unbelievers to discard God's truth and treat what He has created with contempt, this should not be so among Christians. We may opt-out of man-made institutions like the Red Hat Society or AAA, but there are certain institutions that were made by God Himself. The divorce rate would surely decline if this principle were realized.

Day 11

ARRANGING PRIORITIES

"But seek ye first the kingdom of God,
and His righteousness; and all these things
shall be added unto you. " —Matthew 6:33

All of us have many things that put demands upon that precious commodity that we call "time". There are the three R's: Relaxation, Recreation, and Responsibilities. We have things to do at work, in the home, the church, and in the community. From shopping to shaving, it never seems to end. We entangle ourselves so often with so many things that the Lord usually gets the short end of the stick. Have you ever been overwhelmed in the midst of your circumstances and did not know what to do next? Our lives can quickly become a mess when we do not structure our priorities according to the wise principles in the Bible.

Consider our text above as the most important priority list a believer can follow. It's obvious our Lord knew that we would be misguided in this life. He knows what lies within the heart of man, and has provided a way of escape from all the chaos that we get ourselves into. He gives us the roadmap for successful Christian living. He tells us how to set our hearts and affections. He wants to give us a clean sweep and a fresh renewal of grace for the abundant life. It is of utmost importance to seek with our hearts the kingdom of God. Now the kingdom of God is not some futuristic celestial city. Our citizenship is already there and we long to go there, but our priority is not getting to heaven now. The Lord has left us on the earth with a mission and a purpose.

We are commanded to evangelize the lost and advance the kingdom of God on earth. Entrance into the kingdom of God is the new birth. The kingdom of God is the church, both local and universal. The kingdom of God is within us. Christ is our King and as such, He reigns in the hearts of His children. Something is severely amiss in our life when the local church ministry is not a priority.

Attendance upon the assembling of ourselves together should be more and more a priority as we see the day approaching. Activity and involvement will be required of us on the last day. All of us have been given talents and the one that buries them will be called wicked. We should do good to all men, but especially to those who are of the household of faith. We should place a priority on the stated meetings for prayer to bear the burdens of our brethren in Christ. We should seek to support our local church, so that the Pastors will be encouraged as they proclaim God's truth.

It is not enough simply to work, sleep, and believe. We must have priorities that reflect a biblical worldview. I am often asked why I go to church so many times in one week? Is this not what our Lord requires of us? For me, this is part of seeking first the kingdom of God. The local church has a priority of my time, my efforts, and my heart. When she hurts, I hurt. When she calls a fast, I fast. I love Christ, and cannot help but have a love for His bodily bride.

Christ came to save His people, and they make up His church. She is the reason why He went to the cross. Now this is not a priority of external behavior apart from any inward holy motivation. We are said to seek first not only the kingdom of God, but also His righteousness. What the second requirement demands is often overlooked. His righteousness is man's primary need. We need the righteousness of Christ to be saved, and we need His righteousness on a daily basis. Our righteousness must never become a righteousness of our own. We must look to Christ to be saved and continually sanctified.

Day 12

SOLA SCRIPTURA FOR DUMMIES

"According as his divine power hath given unto us
all things that pertain unto life and godliness."
—2 Peter 1:3

The sufficiency of the Bible alone seems to be constantly challenged. The scientific world thought that carbon-dating would be a death blow for the infallibility of the Word of God. If a rock was scientifically proven to have the substance and appearance of carbon that was aged for millions of years, then the earth must be billions of years old. The Scriptures themselves tell us that Adam was created by God to have a body that had aged already! Since God can make a body that has the substance of aged material as in Adam, then He can also make a rock that appears to have aged for billions of years.

Why do we have this need to look outside the Bible for Truth? The Bible ought to be called the Truth book. Our text tells us that it contains all that we need that will ever pertain to this life and how to live it in a godly way. Christianity was not completely in the dark about psychology until Pavlov and Freud came to the rescue! We do not need a book from Dr. Phil for answers to life's issues. Any and all godly advice that is wise and pure comes from above. God has given us all things, as opposed to some things, that pertain to this life and godliness. The Bible is enough. It is the mother book of all books. It is the measuring stick of all supposed wisdom.

When Oprah speaks in opposition to the Bible, she is wrong. If government officials contradict the Scriptures as to what is right, we will still be on the side of Absolute Truth. It is said that the Bible was written by men. That is not completely true! It was written by holy men as they were moved by the Holy Spirit. The Bible was taken out of public schools, yet it is the mother book of History! The Scriptures tell us how to live upright in the home, the workplace, and in the community. It shows us how to handle all of the difficulties that life can throw at us.

It is the Word of God we are to hide in our hearts to help us with temptation. The Scripture is the Christians sword for the rough battles of life. It is both a sharp and double-edged sword. It shows us the importance of guarding our hearts from which flows all the issues of life. Now, it is not enough to have another person state, "Here I stand". We must personally stand on the Scripture alone for salvation, as well as for our ongoing sanctification. If we are going to grow in grace, we must take the milk of the word and eat it as honey.

Since "The Bible Alone" is the source of grace and truth, then we must be very careful about using anything else as such! It is not enough to have a single chapter and verse for everything, so I seek to find two or three more as witnesses! I can recall my good Pastor friend speaking on the subject of marriage. He asked if we ever thought about why the Minister states, "Now you may kiss the bride!" after the vows were exchanged? This traditional service got its tradition from the Bible. The Bible teaches that young men and women should not be kissing before marriage. Culture and tradition are good to have, but not at the expense of what is pure. As followers of Christ, we want to please him with a heart that pants for the righteousness that is found in His Word.

God desires for us to know His truth and to live by it. We do not need modern psychology to be complete and sufficiently able to handle life's problems. God has given us all things that pertain to our life and how to live it out in a way that glorifies Him right in His holy Word.

Day 13

PROPER PASTORAL ESTEEM

"And we beseech you, brethren, to know them
which labour among you, and are over you in
the Lord, and admonish you; And to esteem
them very highly in love for their work's sake."
— 1 Thessalonians 5:12-13

Christ is the great Shepherd of His sheep, but has
charged some men to labor under Him in this great
work. What vocational calling is higher than taking care
of eternal souls? It is the Pastor's work to care for the soul
of the bride of Christ. It is one with great responsibility
and worthy of high esteem. The one that has been gifted
with a Shepherd's heart is made known to the brethren.

The Christian can sense a man with a tender heart and
an ability to handle accurately the Word of Truth. The
Pastor is not one who labors above his people, but among
them. He lives within their midst. He is also a sinner. He

prays with them as well as for them. He eats with them, shares in their joys and weeps with them in their sorrow. He works hard at preaching and teaching the Word. The goal of his instruction is to have his people lovingly obey Christ from a pure heart. It is his role to be given to hospitality. He is to see to it that widows and orphans are properly cared for. He needs to be aware of what is going on, not just in the midst of the world and the universal church, but particularly his own flock over which He has been placed. He is the one appointed at the gatehouse to protect the sheep from wolves and false doctrine.

Christ is the Great Physician and the Pastor is our Physician's Assistant. He is one that is well schooled in Christ. He must be one that has obviously been with Jesus and not a novice. He will have speech that is properly seasoned with grace. He will have a Spirit of love and compassion for the brethren. He will love his wife and train his children well. He will manage his own house well and know how to conduct himself in the house of God. He was called to be an example to the brethren.

We should see him role-modeling the Christian life. He will be rightly dividing the truth in the counseling room, as well as the pulpit. The words that he speaks will be a source of life, and a means of grace for his hearers. Now with his work comes a stricter judgment. This unique man understands that he will one day stand before Christ, and give an account for how he used his talents to feed, lead, and care for the people of God.

Should not work such as this be worthy of double honor? Should such an ox be muzzled as he plows in the midst of such a field as the hearts of God's people? What value can be placed upon one that is called by Christ to this most important and holy task? Consider the text for this day and notice the authority of the office. Pastors are an authority over you in the Lord. He that has all authority has commissioned them. They are not to lord over you like Diotrephese, yet they are not to merely sit back and allow the congregation to rule itself. Jesus rules His church through Pastors that love His people.

With this authority comes accountability and responsibility. Elders must rule well. How much would it be worth for one to have a very skilled Physician at our disposal at any time? Pastors are God's gifts to the church. Though some are dead, yet they still speak in their writings. How are we to view these men? What should our attitudes be towards these servants? Our text tells us to hold them in high esteem. Not because they are better than others, but for the sake of the work that they do. They are Ministers of Souls that have been sent by Christ Himself to do such a work.

Day 14

PARENTING WITH PURPOSE

"And thou shalt teach them diligently unto
thy children, and shalt talk of them when
thou sittest in thine house, and when thou
walkest by the way, and when thou liest down,
and when thou risest up."
—Deuteronomy 6:7

Children are a direct blessing from God Himself. Only
divine providence can open a womb and make a human
soul. There are no accidents or mistakes with God. Allow
me to share some secular views of children that are completely contrary to that of Christianity. There is a view
that children are a curse. Though not articulated with
that terminology, here is the implication. The pregnancy
prevention business is a billion dollar one. Why would
we want to prevent what God has called such a blessing?

Some people fear that children will ruin their finances.
Money is chosen as an idol above the Lord's will. "Chil-

dren", it is argued, "will cost too much!" and "A baby will interfere with my ability to make money." Now we all need money to live and it is irresponsible to have children without a means to provide for them. I will not give my daughter away to a man who cannot provide for her and her children. However, the reason for making money should be to provide for children God gracioulsy gives us.

It is often greed and idolatry that leads couples to forestall or outrightly refuse to be blessed with children. The lust for money is at the root of viewing children as an inconvenience or as an unnecessary expense. It is a display of depravity when we call evil what God calls good. Some view children as a curse to their social lives. A parent will not be able to freely come and go as they wish with the added burden of caring for a child. The child is viewed as a chain of imprisonment, a punishment, or a "cramp" in one's style of living. In a day when people worship their physique, a pregnancy is seen as the ruin of many years of exercise. It is a business in itself for women in third-world countries to carry the child of another woman that does not wish to go through what she considers a "body-wrecking" pregnancy. To such women, child-bearing is seen as a curse, rather than the beautiful experience of fulfilling a God-given blessing and the extraordinary bonding experience with their infant that attends it.

Once we accept the blessing that it is to have children, we must know what to do with them. You must have an itinerary for these bundles of never-ending energy, or their bouncing off the walls will make you bounce off the walls. Some have children to work in their sweatshops. Some have children to collect more financial assistance. The Christian is to be different. Believing parents are to provide their children with food, shelter, love and education. We are to protect them from the many dangers in this life. We must seek to be an example to them.

It is rightly said, "More is caught than taught." Proverbs 22:6 teaches: "Train up a child in the way he should go; and when he is old, he will not depart from it." This is not a promise to believing parents that if they teach their children right it will guarantee the salvation and sanctification of their children. Many children have been faithfully trained up by mature and godly parents, only to deny the faith and live like the world. This promise is that your children will never forget the way in which you taught them. Even though they rebel, they will recall the Christian way of life that was carefully lived out before them. Parents are to provide, protect, pray for, and train up their children in Christ by example.

Day 15

THE STRONG MAN IS BOUND

"How can one enter into a strong man's house,
and spoil his goods, except he first bind
the strong man?" —Matthew 12:29

The Lord Jesus was in the "devil-casting-out" business. His main desire and work is to root out evil from the hearts of His people. In our text the strong man is Satan. Satan is not a weak man. He is likened in Scripture to that of a Lion as opposed to a mere mouse. Let us notice from our text that this strong man has a house and goods. The Devil is the ruler of this present visible world order that exists outside of Christ. That is to say it's reasons for doing whatever it does is not to glorify Jesus Christ. The unbelievers are Satan's "goods". They are of their father the devil. He holds them captive in unbelief and seeks to use and control them.

Satan uses various means to keep people from God and the truth of His word. Our text tells us that these goods cannot be taken from the strong man until his power is taken away. He must be gagged and bound if his goods will be loosed. This shows how stubborn and rebellious he is. He will not submit to the authority of another, even if it is God Himself. He has so much pride, the very thing that was the cause of his fall. He has a firm grip upon sinners and will not let them go without a violent war.

That is why Satan must be completely subdued. He must be continuously bound because his heart still desires to hold onto those goods. Once let loose, he will seek to destroy what has been taken if he cannot have them for himself. Though sadly there is no shortage of "end-days" heresies, you can be sure of one thing: when Christ died on the cross Satan was bound! Jesus crushed the head of the serpent and broke the chains of bondage to sin that held the sinner captive to Satan, to sin and to death. Thanks be to God that sin can no longer have dominion over those who believe.

This binding was both immediate and prolonged. It was evil that held captive the souls of men. Jesus shed His blood and made an atonement that opened the gates of heaven immediately. Our Old Covenant brethren looked forward to redemption and their entrance into heaven was by faith in a future work of the Messiah. This binding of the strong man, which Christ accomplished on the cross, also opened the pearly gates for all of us who now look back to that most blessed event in human history.

When Jesus said, "It is finished", He very well could have said, "Satan is now bound". It was the complete obedience of Christ that was the requirement of God for sinners to have entrance into spiritual life. Many times the Lord revealed his commands, telling man to keep them and live. Because of sin, in Adam, we all fell from grace and became slaves to Satan. He had us bound, and the only hope for us would be for one that is much stronger to, in turn, bind him up. As strong as the serpent can be, he is no match for the Lion of Judah!

Now this binding is a work that has its power and beginning in Christ, but is also meant to be continued through us. Matthew 16:19 says: "I will give unto thee the keys of the kingdom of heaven: and whatsoever thou shalt bind on earth shall be bound in heaven". Our power to partake in the ongoing binding of Satan is not from within ourselves, but is the power and authority of Christ. This power enables us to snatch others from the flames of Hell. It is what enables us to overcome temptation and sin. The world may say, "The Devil made me do it", but the Christian has no such excuse to not live a godly life that conforms to Christ and His word. Remember well Romans 6:14: "Sin shall not have dominion over you."

Day 16

BOOMERANG HAMARTIOLOGY

"But if ye will not do so, behold,
ye have sinned against the LORD,
and be sure your sin will find you out."
— Numbers 32:23

What is your hamartiology? Well, hamartiology is just a big word theologians use for the truth regarding sin (hamartia is greek for sin, or literally "to miss the mark"). Do you live practically with the notion that some of your sins are a secret from God? We should all know that God is omniscient (all-knowing) and omnipresent (present everywhere). It was a foolish mindset that led Adam to hide from the presence of the Lord after he sinned. Jonah also thought that he could flee from the Lord's presence. In the New Testament we have examples of Annanias and Saphira trying to hide their sin from the Holy Ghost. The Psalmist knew that if he were to go down to Hell that God is there.

A boomerang is fun to play with, but can be very dangerous. You can throw it as hard as you can, and it will come back to smite you if you are not careful! Is this not the nature of Sin? There are consequences to sin that are not worthy to be compared with that of righteousness. Now we must acknowledge that sin does have pleasure for a season. The Christian can enjoy sin, but only for a season. That season is often very short lived. We might go to David as he was grieving the loss of his child and ask him if his fornication and murder was worth it?

How about the prodigal son that had his time of indulging in the depraved acts of unbelievers. Listen; "What happens in Vegas..." does *not* stay in Vegas. I can recall a man that went to Vegas for a billiards tournament. He returned home, but only for his wife to find the phone number of the woman he temporarily used as his companion. I have four brothers and we chuckle as we reminisce about our teenage days. We shared the same room and when a brother came home late smelling like a brewery, Mom always woke before he could sneak into bed. She'd get a whiff of the alcohol stench and ask my barely conscious brother, "Have you been drinking?"

The Lord is not mocked, and we do reap what we sow. This is why the Lord tells us not to be deceived. Sin is very deceptive in nature. It seems easy to believe that we can live our lives apart from God's revealed will, and get away with it. The carpet can seemingly hide the filth, but it is not before long that we trip, stumble and fall over what we tried to hide. Now, there are sins that are hidden to men's eyes, but as the song goes, "His eye is on the sparrow, and I know He's watching me". God is not hiding in the back, waiting for us to sin. He is in the front, seeking to lead us into the paths of righteousness for His name's sake. He stands at the door of our hearts and knocks with a desire to come in and enjoy fellowship with us.

We sin when we refuse to take his hand and counsel. His need to judge sin in our lives is not a source of pleasure for Him. We incur the consequences when we rebel. This does not mean that the consequences will happen right away. They are sure to come, but maybe not right away. Being physically healthy and financially prosperous is not evidence of being right with God. The cry of the Psalmist was, "Why do the wicked prosper?" Psalm 7:11-12: "God judgeth the righteous, and God is angry with the wicked every day. If he turn not, he will whet his sword; he hath bent his bow, and made it ready."

Notice that this readiness to judge sin is not only for the wicked. The righteous is a designation for believers. If we live healthy and financially prosperous while holding on to sin, we can be sure that our sin will find us out when we give an account to Christ.

Day 17

RECAPTURING FELLOWSHIP

"And they continued steadfastly in the apostles'
doctrine and fellowship, and in breaking of bread,
and in prayers." —Acts 2:42

In most circles today "fellowship" has been reduced to
a spread of refreshments after worship service. Let us notice that our text makes a distinction between fellowship
and breaking of bread. This kind of fellowship is something that every Christian has with God, and one another.
It is also something in which each believer should continue steadfastly. When Christ died, He brought down all
walls of partition that separated His people. Socially, eco-
nomically, and ethnically there will still be differences,
but they should not separate the people of God. We have
been made into one body.

In Christ there is neither Yankee nor Confederate,
all are one in communion with God and thus with one
another. There are not two bodies of Christ on earth. He

does not have two flocks. We are one in position as brothers and sisters. This position is meant to be extremely practical. Brothers and sisters should have a special loving relationship with each other. They should enjoy one another's company and seek the higher value of another, even at their own expense. The family gatherings should be sweet experiences of giving and receiving love. We ought to know the needs and hurts of one another in a very intimate way.

How can we bear one another's burdens if we don't even know them? Our speech should seek to edify the brethren and minister to their circumstances. A word can only be fitly spoken in the context of understanding the needs of our brethren. It is often overlooked that the New Testament church was essentially a group of believers that met primarily in homes. They were not out for an hour of good music and a story to touch the heart. Their fellowship was grass roots and meaningful. They were in the midst of extreme persecution and needed all the comfort and encouragement that they could get. They were in the midst of a war that claimed the very lives of many of their precious families.

Oh friend, are we not in the midst of a battle as well? Are there not hurting people in the halls of our local church? God loves all infants, but has given them moms to properly care for them. As an infant needs much more than milk if it is to grow into a healthy and complete individual, so every child of God needs the grace of Christian fellowship. There are souls that are craving the intimacy and nurture of a few others that sincerely care about them. I had a good Christian friend tell me that he had found a better sense of fellowship on a barstool at his local pub during his unsaved years than with a group of cold-hearted and independent believers at church.

My friends, friendship with the world can appear to be attractive if we do not have friendship within the church. This is why fellowship needs to be steadfastly continued. The Devil loves to tempt us away from Christ and His church with non-believing fellowship. This is why the apostle warns us about becoming unequally yoked together with unbelievers. Though there is a sense of fellowship, it is a counterfeit one. Christians still have the remnants of the flesh. The bad company of unbelievers will crave any remaining sin in the heart of a believer. We need to foster opportunities to get together in small groups for close fellowship with like-minded brothers and sisters in Christ.

The corporate nature of the church demands that we use our homes to fan the flames of fellowship. It isn't enough to come out from among unbelievers; we must be intimately involved in the fellowship of the brethren.

Day 18

AUTONOMY ABUSED

"I wrote unto the church: but Diotrephes, who loveth to have the preeminence among them, receiveth us not. Wherefore, if I come, I will remember his deeds which he doeth, prating against us with malicious words: and not content therewith, neither doth he himself receive the brethren, and forbiddeth them that would, and casteth them out of the church."

—3 John 1:9-10

The Scriptures teach us that Christ's local churches should work together. Everywhere we turn, we find local churches helping and cooperating with other churches of like faith. Each one maintained its autonomy (was not governed by another church or denomination), but worked together for the common good and advancement of the Gospel. The independent nature of the local church is a Biblical concept that has become completely abused. Some churches are so independent, its as if they are alone and separated from the universal church. Such a cult-like spirit needs to be addressed.

Christ has given each local church authority, and each their own set of keys to bind and loose. However, each church is supposed to work with other sister churches and maintain accountability. This is why the transfer of members from one church to another has until recently always been done by letters. Each local, bible-believing, church is called to recognize the authority of the other. More and more, we are seeing churches that have violated this concept. In our text, we have a pastor, Diotrephes, failing to receive the Apostles. He did not accept them as genuine co-laborers that Christ had Himself appointed and established. He also did not receive the missionary brethren that were sent out by another church to work along his side.

This practice of isolation made matters worse for his local church. He forbade his people from supporting, or being involved with these missionaries. If his members did work with them, they were thrown out of the church! There are many problems with Diotrephes, but the one that stands out as most highly prevalent today is this: He had a very narrow view of the church. He was very closed to working with other churches. I think I understand part of the reason why so many churches have become isolated. There was a time when denominational organization was on the rise. It was the norm for churches to fellowship and cooperate together and to coordinate themselves in denominational affiliations. Then some denominations began to threaten the autonomy of their local churches. Pastors were appointed without congregational approval. Missionary funds were used for things which member churches found objectionable. When the troubles became heightened, the denomination acted as a tyrant and sought to rule over the local church. Some local churches even pursued the heathen courts to keep their monies and buildings!

These long and soul-sucking battles caused roots of bitterness that lead to a fear of getting hurt again. Thus, many local churches took to hiding in their ecclesiastical shell. Church polity was the new crusade, and her banner became Independent with a capital I! There was no longer an eye for the bigger picture of the universal church. Many churches limited the great commission only to their little local "Jerusalem" and justified it with a special "Missions Weekend" once a year. It is not enough to give sporadic missions offerings. Obedience to the Great Commission requires the acknowledgment of, and participation with, other biblically faithful churches.

Day 19

PRAYER FORMATION

"Praying always with all prayer and supplication in the Spirit." —Ephesians 6:18

The practice of habitual prayer will bring reformation in the heart and life of a believer. The Apostle has told us that we do not pray as we ought. It was a mark of humility for Jesus' disciple to ask, "Lord, teach us to pray?" We have so many battles that we cannot afford to lapse in this means of grace. Prayer is two-way communication with God. It is so often reduced to a one-way grocery list of requests. We give them to God like some kind of Christmas list. We need to be still and seek to hear the voice and counsel of God when we pray.

Samuel learned this lesson when Eli made him sensitive to this reality. The Lord can only hear the prayers of His children and only honors them when their hearts are pure and free from sin. Though His common grace rains down upon the just and the unjust, there is special grace for the repentant in heart. David said that if he regarded iniquity in his heart, the Lord would not hear his prayers. Prayer is not a ritualistic recital as if we will be heard for our many words. Even when we do not know how to articulate with words, the Spirit of God intercedes for us with groaning that cannot be uttered. Consider the model life of the Lord Jesus and note how often he would get to a place by Himself to pray.

There is private prayer, and there is corporate prayer. God dwells within each and every believer, but promises His presence in a very special way with two or more that gather in His name. There are certain obstacles that can only be overcome by the ministry of prayer. There are certain demons that just will not come out unless God's people pray. We often hear of the need for revival. It is usually in context to the condition of the world and the need for evangelism but Biblical revival is something that happens inside the church. It has to do with sanctification in the hearts of God's people.

Revival is birthed and nurtured by the ministry of prayer. *"If My people, which are called by My name, shall humble themselves, and pray, and seek My face, and turn from their wicked ways; then will I hear from heaven, and will forgive their sin, and will heal their land."* (2Chronicles 7:14) When Christians begin to get right with God and seek Him and His will with prayer, it will affect them and all around them. Prayer is the fuel that feeds the flames of grace. Prayer is the circuit that gives power for the abundant life. Prayer can be the difference between having and not having, but we must pray with the right motives.

The motivation for prayer is very important. The Christian must ask for what will glorify God. We want the will of Christ in all things. We want to see people saved. We want to see churches birthed. We want to see sound doctrine proclaimed. We want to see Christians living holy lives. We want to be filled with the joy of the Lord. We want to be a good testimony of the Gospel that saved us. We want the light of God's grace to permeate the church and expose the darkness of the world in which we live. We want what can only be obtained through the ministry of prayer. This is why we are commanded to pray at all times with all sorts of prayer.

We should pray to adore Christ, confess our sin, give thanks for past and present blessings, and to plead with the Lord of the harvest to send forth more laborers into this field that is ripe and ready to be shaken and turned upside down for Him.

Day 20

PASTORAL PRIORITIES

"Then the twelve called the multitude of the disciples unto them, and said, it is not reason that we should leave the word of God, and serve tables. Wherefore brethren look ye out among you seven men of honest report, full of the Holy Ghost and wisdom, whom we may appoint over this business. But we will give ourselves continually to prayer, and to the ministry of the word." —Acts 6:2-4

I was asked to be a guest preacher for a church that had just lost its pastor. I asked what had happened to this dear servant? He was gracious in character and solid in his doctrine. I was told that he had been an automobile mechanic before his calling to the ministry. The Deacons said that he had been giving too much time to fixing the cars of his people. It interfered with his pastoral duties and the church ministry suffered greatly. Now, I'm not suggesting it's a sin for a pastor to help a member fix their car, but something is wrong with the priorities of the pastor when fixing cars takes precedence over his ministerial priorities.

When another church lost their pastor I was again asked to fill the pulpit. Of course I asked what had happened to this dear servant? The Deacons proceeded to tell me that he had a good singing voice and had been devoting his time to building his singing ministry. He would go on tour and call his church from the road to let them know that he will not make the Sunday worship service because he would be singing elsewhere that Lord's Day!

Good men that love the Lord have fallen prey to the "priority demon". Perhaps they just became remiss, or maybe they were not trained properly in this area. Regardless of why, this was their downfall, and it brought much pain and trouble to the cause of Christ and the health of His Church.

The responsibilities of a pastor are many. He must be given to hospitality. He is to oversee all the ministries of the church. He must have a hands-on approach to what others are teaching and how they are living. He is to be a good listener and a compassionate counselor. He is responsible for the proper care of his wife, as well as his church. He must wash her with the water of the word so that she might become more and more holy. He must pray for and with his family. He must train up his children when he rises and when he lies down. He must take heed unto his own soul with self-examination and mortification of his deeds of the flesh. He has many responsibilities, but our text focuses on a Biblical view of what his priority should be. Prayer and the ministry of the word are the two areas that cannot be neglected. They are to take up the majority of his time and efforts.

Notice in our text that it is not appropriate that a pastor neglect the ministry of the word to serve tables. He must be a servant, but such service must be in study and teaching above all else. While other service may be lawful, it is not profitable if it causes a neglect of the ministry of the word as priority. He is first and foremost a student of Christ, and it is his role to proclaim God's truth with authority and compassion. This must be the desire of his heart.

Along with this desire, he must understand the importance of prayerfully entreating God for special unction in the public proclamation of the Word. He must understand that preaching is the primary means of grace whereby souls are saved and sanctified, but he must also know that without prayer his ministry of the word would be without power.

Day 21

THE ORIGIN OF LIFE

"The birth of Jesus was on this wise: When His
mother Mary was espoused to Joseph,
before they came together, she was found with
child of the Holy Ghost." —Matthew 1:18

Have you ever been moved by the media coverage
of neglected children? Sadly, I recall more than a few
news reports about a newborn baby being found dead
in a garbage pail or dumpster! While such tragic crimes
are rightly considered illegal, there are countless other
"legal" atrocities executed daily under the banner of pro-
choice abortions. The law of the land has clashed with the
law of God on this matter. The Christian right is usually
marginalized as being old-school traditionalists that are
just out of touch with modern society.

The mainstream media portrays pro-lifers as political
opponents that are close-minded and judgmental as they

stand on streets with picket signs, and hatefully con-
demn the "right" (so-called) of a woman to terminate
her unwelcome pregnancy. Why are these Christian
protesters so determined in their war against abortion? Well, let's first point out that, in their vehemence,
some believers have erred on the side of arrogance or
even hatred in their pursuit to defend what they believe to be true.

Jesus desires the world to know that we are His disciples by our love. Love has been blurred by the emotional overload. Whatever the believer does, it must
be done to the glory of God. God is not glorified when
His people show bitterness and hatred towards others.
When picketing is done with the wrong spirit it does
not bring glory to God! Christians are supposed to be
submissive to the powers that be, even when they are
told to clear the sidewalk. If I were to shout "the earth
is round" with anger and hatred, it may be speaking
the truth, but not in love.

Although many abortion protesters have abused
their efforts at speaking truth, abortion is still wrong.
Not because this is my political opinion, but because
God has revealed it in His Word. *Thou shalt not murder* is violated whenever an abortion takes place. The
debate over when life begins is severely challenged
by our text. Before the belly of Mary even began to
enlarge, she is said to be found with child! Modern-
day distinctions like fetus or embryo, often made
to diminish the value of the life in question, are not

found in Scripture. The life of the child began when she conceived. The Bible does not call it a piece of tissue, but a child.

An unborn child has been endowed by its Creator with certain unalienable rights. Whether there was a rape or the mother's life is in danger, the two most frequently argued justifications for abortion, the child in the womb has a right to life. The reality is that millions of women have had abortions and it would be extremely difficult for them to acknowledge that they took the life of their own child! It is easier to willingly deceive themselves and suppress the reality about their choice to abort when the child can be dismissed as "only a piece of tissue".

While that may be the choice of the unbeliever, the Christian has a conscience that is bound by the Word of God. We must stand before Christ one day and give an account for what we say and what we did in this life. It is at His throne that the gavel will come down on the side of truth. So what do we do with the one that chose to abort their child but now has sincere remorse? Is this not why Christ came into the world and shed His blood on the cross? He came to call all sinners to repentance. He came to save His people from their sins.

Abortion is a sin for which Christ died. He will cleanse and bring healing to the broken and contrite. He will also use, as an agent for truth on this issue, and as a minister to countless others, the one that comes to understand their sin of abortion. This, my dear friend, is a truth that saves lives! The Bible tells us that the blood of the innocent cries out from the ground. May this truth promote the dignity of life and bring healing to many hearts.

Day 22

DEMOCRACY OR THEOCRACY?

"Then Peter and the other apostles
answered and said, we ought to obey God
rather than men." —Acts 5:29

American culture has made an idol of "Majority Rule". Whatever the majority of the people support, it becomes a law. While God ordains the powers of government, they are not given authority to override the supreme authority of God. The unbeliever may be emboldened by whatever is culturally or politically "correct", but the Christian looks to the Word of the Lord. The Christian is to respect all authority and be submissive to such so long as there is not a clashing with the authority of the Lord. Whenever there is a clashing of authority, the Christian must always yield Scripture.

In the context of our text we see the government seeking to silence Christians. This is not an isolated case in the history of the church. Many governments have sought to slay the truth and suppress it with the sword of law. The believers in our text understood that the word of God is their ultimate rule. They had a conscience that was bound by Scripture. You may recall when the Israelites wanted a King. The Lord through Samuel sought to show them that a king was not where they should be looking for societal stability. Well, the "majority ruled", and the Lord granted them the King they strove for. It was not a happy experience for the people. Why are we so reticent to look to the Lord and rely upon His revealed Word?

Saul was given us as a lesson in politics for the people of God. God will, at times, give what the majority want when they are discontent! You've heard the phrase,— "Be careful what you wish for". I saw a bumper sticker that read, "Don't blame me, I voted for …" When people speak or vote, it is ultimately from their hearts. If the heart is good, good things will come out. The problem arises when we consider that the heart of man outside of Christ is deceitful and desperately wicked. All that we speak needs to be held in check by the Word of God, which is pure.

The Bible is what needs to be used to examine our thoughts, views, and actions. Just because an opinion has a majority of support, it does not make it right; remember Hitler had a majority support from his people! Now don't misunderstand; it is best when people have a say in how they are governed. It is good to have a society, a government and a political system wherein the voice of the people can be heard. It is good for folks to have a freedom of speech, but not to contradict the speech that came from God as revealed in His Word! Where is God's freedom to speak? I trust you've heard the expression: "Opinions are like belly buttons… everyone has one!" Can you imagine a belly button commentary on the Bible! Opinions are good to contemplate, but must be ultimately submissive to the Word of God

Let the pundits have their opinions, but as for us, and our house, we must serve the Lord! This problem is not only domestic. Something is flawed in a foreign policy that seeks to spread democracy for democracy's sake as its goal. What good is democracy, if the majority of the people support terrorism? The Christian views democracy as a means and not an end. Let the people speak, but may it be according to the Word of God. Believers should have a Theocratic mindset. God should rule in our hearts, our homes, in our communities, in our nations and in the whole world!

Day 23

POISON IVY LEAGUE

" If thou wilt not observe to do all the words
of this law that are written in this book,
that thou mayest fear this glorious and
fearful name, THE LORD THY GOD;
Then the LORD will make thy plagues
wonderful, and the plagues of thy seed,
great plagues, and sore sicknesses, and
of long continuance." — Deuteronomy 28:58-59

Where would you prefer your attorney to have been educated? Would it be impressive for him to have studied at Harvard, Yale, or Princeton? It might be a surprise for you to study the history of Ivy League Law schools. You will find a Judeo-Christian foundation. You will also find an ethical policy based on the Ten Commandments. Let me tell you what you will not find. Law will not be viewed as relativistic. Lawyers will not be trained to find the loopholes to jump through. The goal of the attorney will not be to get the client off the hook. A biblical view of Law has a goal to seek out the truth and bring about justice.

To be a student of law, one must be a student of truth. How can a lawyer help with justice if there is not a quest for, and understanding of, truth? It seems that the modern motivation for a student to enter law school is the opportunity it affords to make big bucks. There was a time when parents viewed the practice of law as a mission field. They would encourage their children to become lawyers to help people. The Christian attorney can fight to uphold, support and defend truth. They can rise to aid the one who was taken advantage of.

God has ordained the powers that be. The judicial system has a divine purpose to reward the good and punish the wicked. Whenever an attorney embarks upon the pursuit of frivolous lawsuits, he does so in complete opposition to God. Let me illustrate the absurdity of what goes on under the banner of supposed justice. Let's take a man and his drive-thru breakfast nightmare. He gets scolded with 2nd degree burns and wants a million dollars from the fast food corporation that sold him his hot cup of coffee. Now you understand, the morning breakfast run happens soon after one awakes. Even a morning person is not fully aware before breakfast, not to mention they're still without the caffeine kick they get from their coffee. So here you have a man not as awake as he should be, driving his car, and trying to buy and eat his breakfast behind the wheel! How about the distraction of the car radio going as the man grabs his change and asks for salt and napkins? Instead of placing the scalding coffee in the cup holder, the man places it between his legs!

Can you hear the soundtrack to the movie Jaws: dun-don, dun-don, dun-don! He squeezes his legs together just a little too hard and off shoots the lid along with a volcanic eruption of scalding java-lava in the lap of this man that instantly wishes he was back in bed. Is there an attorney that can help this poor man win the frivolous lawsuit lottery? Unfortunately there's a line out the door. If he had purchased his coffee from the local street-cart vendor what lawyer would accept his case but it's revealed that the coffee was purchased from a major corporation, so the dollar signs spell— ka-ching, ka-ching.

Can I suggest that there is a link between attorneys that haven't a care about truth and the schools that trained them? We wanted God and His Ten Commandments out of our courts and schools, and then we wonder why we have a godless judicial system of moral injustice. If the Ivy League school disregards the Judeo-Christian foundation of conservative moral right, then they will train their students to be liberal, left, and immoral.

Day 24

CONSTITUTIONAL CONSISTENCY

"So God created man in His own image, in the image of God created He him; male and female created He them." —Genesis 1:27

Here we have part of the founding document of all mankind. This verse was not only written for Americans. God created all people in his own image. Dignity and respect for the Creator is what compels us to give dignity and respect to what He has created. It is consistent for us to share in God's general love for the entire world and the least of His children. Our constitution or make-up as image bearers necessitates a sincere concern for each and every person that God has created.

There is not a supreme race or nation that has been given divine sanction to look down upon any other. From North Dakota to Mongolia, all are equal in worth and value. The American Constitution addresses and embraces this perspective. Our very Declaration of Independence states, "All people have been endowed by their

Creator with certain unalienable rights". As an American, one cannot deny Creation without a blatant desecration of its founding documents.

That a "Creator" is the origin of mankind is both implicit and explicit! You've probably seen the Christian fish symbol (icthus) with legs on it that supporters of evolutionary dogma display on their cars as their way to mock us poor ignorant fools who believe what God has said on the matter. They smack the God of creation in the face, but why don't they burn the American flag while they're at it. Constitutional America accepts that God has created all people. The Christian view of creation is not only logical, but also consistent with what both the Scriptures declare and the birth certificate of America upholds.

Our founding fathers also penned that whenever the God-given unalienable rights of His created people are violated, "it becomes necessary for one people to dissolve the political bands" of such that do so. "Whenever any form of Government becomes destructive to these ends, it is the Right of the People to alter or to abolish it, and to institute new Government". "When a long train of abuses…. It is their right, it is their duty, to throw off such Government, and to provide new Guards for their future security". What should be the Christian response to governments that are destructive towards the unalienable rights of their people?

It may not be politically correct to use the label "axis of evil", but is it not evil to beat women on the street for talking to a man? Is it not evil to forbid Christian evangelism and missionary activity, while enforcing the spread of hateful and terroristic radical Islamic propaganda? Is it not evil when a leader relieves himself on a toilet made of gold while his people starve for lack of daily bread? How about denying the holocaust and publicly stating that Israel should be wiped off the face of the earth? While such hateful threats were once written off as middle-eastern rhetoric, after they've flown our own jetliners as suicide bombers upon our soil, murdering thousands and inflicting terror upon millions, maybe it's time to start being consistent to the principles of our founding documents.

Can I suggest that there are circumstances that make it necessary to dissolve such political bands? When those circumstances arise, it is our duty to throw off such government, and to provide new guards for their future security! This is not only for the domestic policy of early colonial America. The constitution of mankind demands that we uphold the dignity and respect that God has created all people with.

Day 25

BORN HOMOSEXUAL?

"Thou shalt not lie with mankind,
as with womankind:
it is abomination." — Leviticus 18:22

A homosexual couple began attending the church I pastored. As usual, I sought to do the work of an evangelist. During appropriate times, I would stress the importance of holiness and repentant faith in Christ. After the first service, we exchanged casual greetings before they left. I thought that they sensed the tone of our ministry and would not desire to come back. To my surprise, they returned a second time. I did not want to offend them with truth in the absence of love. I sought to be extra gracious and cordial towards them to establish a loving relationship and win them to Christ. The Deacon Committee did not share the same approach.

There was a concern that they were attending to take over the church, and propagate their agenda! I was pressured to ask them to not attend under the banner of "It does not look good to the community" and "It is as if we have embraced them and are now encouraging that life-style." I pled with the deacons to allow them to sit under the Word of God and hear the Gospel. My rationale was that they were not members and only attended. If we did not allow sinners in to hear the Word, we would never have conversions!

I visited these two men in their home. I brought a good book as a gift and asked if I could pray with them. The older one then declared that he was a homosexual and asked about my views. I cautiously told him that the Bible calls it sin, but I would seek to continue to show love to him and seek to help him grow in the Christian faith. He came to see me in my office a few weeks later and told me that he wanted to publicly repent and join the church. He then confessed that he was a born-again Christian and had served in the Pastoral ministry for several years.

We counseled together many times and I sought to help him through this big step in his life. He began to share with me how his deliverance was an ongoing daily need. He said he believed that he was born with this particular problem of sin and that even after becoming born-again, it remained a daily struggle. I was always of the mindset that this was a chosen lifestyle and those who say that they were made like that only seek to blame God for their behavior. This was not the case with this man. It was his opinion that he was born with a sinful nature like everyone. He viewed his struggle with homosexuality as a result of that sin problem. He did not blame God for this. As some might be more prone to abuse alcohol, this man's sin of preference was homosexuality. We all have a sin problem, but it can manifest itself in different ways. Some are prone to violent anger, some gambling, and some are prone to rebel by way of homosexuality.

My acquaintance with this man caused me to rethink my position on the matter. I gained a deeper compassion for those who struggle with homosexuality. When a drug addict comes into our midst, they need Christ and His grace daily to resist temptation. The repentant alcoholic also lives by a daily dependence upon Christ for victory. While I fought the tendency to doubt the conversion of someone in a continuing struggle with a particular sin, I had to acknowledge that we all struggle with sin but the temptation to relapse into sin might have a stronger pull for different types of sin.

I no longer dispute that homosexuality could be one sinful appetite a fallen man might be born with, so long as it is not an excuse to justify it. Even though certain sins might be more prevalent, God created man good and can never be blamed for our immoral behavior.

Day 26

CHRISTIAN EXCLUSIVITY

Neither is there salvation in any other: for there is none other name under heaven given among men, whereby we must be saved. —Acts 4:12

How many times have you heard that all religions are good ladders that lead to heaven. Isn't it arrogant to say that your way is the *only* way? What should be the Christian take upon the matter? How would you respond to such sentiments? The Bible tells us that the Christian faith is a very narrow way. There will not be a broad acceptance by a majority. Many will go the other way that leads to death, as the way of Christ (which leads to life) is rejected. There is only one God, and He has provided only one Mediator between Himself and mankind. If any would be saved from their sin and gain entrance into glory, they must come through Christ alone.

Since Jesus is the only mediator, his mother Mary cannot mediate. Though she was blessed amongst women, she is not a co-mediator with her Son. Since Christ is the only Mediator, it is folly to seek mediation from dead saints. Since Christ is the only Mediator, any attempt to approach God outside of sincere repentance and personal faith in Christ is a vain and invalid means. Any prayers thrown up to Heaven apart from Christ will be returned to sender. Good works done apart from receiving Christ will be viewed by God as filthy rags.

While it is good for the unsaved boy scout to walk an old woman across the street, all his good cannot cover his vile rebellion against God unless it is washed in the blood of Jesus. I once sought to encourage a widow who professed to be a Christian. I told her that the Lord has always taken care of her in spite of all her difficulties. She proceeded to let me know that she attained what she has by her own hard work! She evidenced a pride that robbed God of His glory in all her labor. Who gave her the breath, health, and strength to do her work?

I then proceeded to ask her why Christ died? If good works could earn God's favor, then the death of Christ was not necessary and Christ is not the only way! The Christian gospel is not Christ plus Mohammed or Buddha or anything else. Christ alone is the way, the truth and the life. All other ways are wrong ways that lead to death. To espouse that Jesus is the *only* way for one to become right with God is usually perceived by the unbeliever as very narrow minded, bigoted, and arrogant.

May I suggest that there is another way to look at the exclusive claims of Christ? Christians can be thankful and rejoice that God has made it so clear and easy for us to know the way! He did not leave us in the dark as to which way is right. It was very gracious of Him to give us His Word and make it so crystal clear. Search the Scriptures and you will see that they testify of Christ. The entire Bible has a grand running theme and it unfolds the person and work of Jesus from Genesis to Revelation.

The Bible exposes the errors of the false ways. It makes known the light and exposes the darkness. These things have been written about Christ that we might know that we have eternal life. We are not left to guess whether or not we will ultimately make it. It is not a religious lottery. Christianity is God seeking mankind through Christ, whereas *religion* is man hoping to reach God. We can rejoice that there is one certain and sure way for sinners to be made clean and that is through the work of Christ and Christ alone.

Day 27

CHRISTIAN FITNESS

What? Know ye not that your body is the
temple of the Holy Ghost which is in you,
which ye have of God, and ye are not
your own? —1 Corinthians 6:19

As Christians we are called to be a good steward of what the Lord entrusts to us. The health and well-being of our bodies will affect our ability to function. There are many dangers to avoid in how we take care of our bodies. One is the idolatrous nature of fitness addiction. I have owned and operated fitness centers and have seen many people spend way too much time in the gym. Some folks do not even break a sweat, but seem to enjoy the gym atmosphere. There is the allure of profane music and the meat-market quest for eye-candy. The muscle-head Arnold Schwarzenegger "wanna-be" wanders to and fro seeking a mirror to devour after each set.

There is also the eternal treadmill runner seeking the endorphin high. He burns so many calories that his muscular system pleads daily for rest. Now the motivation for the Christian is to glorify God. Christian fitness is about stewardship not personal satisfaction. Neglecting our bodies by lack of exercise and poor eating habits is bad stewardship. The Scriptures call overeating sin. Gluttony is one of those sins that cannot be easily hidden. It is a deed of the flesh that is obvious. My own belly has convicted me many times.

We live in a computerized and mechanized world that has greatly diminished the need for physical manpower. From the forklift to the self-checkout, we all tend to use our bodies less than at any other time in human history. The Bible tells us that bodily exercise profits. Though it profits little in comparison to the importance and benefits of spiritual exercise. Eating healthy food and performing regular exercise are a profitable activities for the Christian. Not only can this please the Great Physician, but it can also please your family physician. The body, mind and spirit will all be healthier. It can prevent depression, relieve stress, maintain blood pressure, and reduce the chance of a multitude of illnesses. You will think better, sleep better and feel better. This will allow a better handling of the daily stress that accompanies life in the home, at the workplace and in the church.

Pursuing fitness does not require a lot of money, time or a bestselling program. We don't need the shiny weights or a personal trainer. You don't need a degree in nutrition to start making healthy eating choices. The simple reduction of caloric intake and the increase of caloric expenditure will do the job. You will do good by replacing the bag of chips with a bag of baby carrots to munch on instead. Gradually cut down on the sugary foods and gradually increase your activity.[2]

A casual walk can progress to a brisk walk or advance to a jog depending on your age and health condition. If the upper body is lacking, take along something in the hands as you go. The typical recommendation of time sufficiency is thirty minutes, three times a week.[3] This is a great time for Scripture meditation, or the utilization of a familiar hymn for private worship. What you sow is what you'll reap. If you sow a decade of corruption in your body, you will reap a body that is more corrupted than what it should be. It does not glorify God when Christians become couch potatoes. We should not need seek to be a Charles Atlas but we should seek to glorify God by how we take care of what he has given to us as good stewards.

---

2 These are general principles and should not be understood to be specific advice to any reader. Consult your doctor and/or nutritionist for specific advice tailored to your health condition.

3 Ask your doctor if you are healthy enough to partake in a regular program of exercise.

Day 28

NO BRAKES!

"Flee also youthful lusts." —2 Timothy 2:22

God is a very wise and compassionate Father. His wisdom compels Him to train up His children well. He has cautioned them in His Word about the many dangers that they would do very well to avoid. The subject of our text is youthful lusts. There is an innate desire for sin even in the heart of a believer. The remnants of the flesh remain and Paul here cautions Pastor Timothy about it. The godly are not immune to the allure of sin. Everywhere one may turn, there is a militant onslaught of all sorts of temptations.

One cannot listen to secular music for long without hearing bedroom psychology. Rated-X imagery has taken over our television screens. The good-ole days of Andy Griffith's Mayberry, the American flag and apple pie have been replaced by a sex, drugs, and rock and roll culture. It is almost impossible to find anyone dressed in modest apparel. Tattoos are strategically placed for others to look with lust. The scarlet letter has changed from A for adultery to V for Virgin. Our culture has gone from premarital sex acceptance to premature sex expectance. Now we should expect all this from the world, but where is the believer in all this?

Unfortunately, this dating game flirtation of lust has crept into the church and goes virtually unchallenged. Whatever happened to that song, *Be careful little eyes what you see— for your Father up above is looking down in Love*? Christian parents have bought into the world's view of courtship. Picture the teenage girl beginning her hormonal cycles and the teenage boy overflowing with testosterone. There they are as gas and spark. They are an accident waiting to happen. However godly they may be, the fallen nature lurks within. Immaturity alone will work against any resolve to resist the desire for intimacy. It's even worse when parents give young people money, the car keys, and allow them hours of freedom outside the home for which they are unaccountable!

Is this not done in Christian homes across our land? The principle implied by the word "Flee" is violated. We are to avoid these temptations. We are to run in the opposite direction of this fire. This is not only for the teenager. The aged can be overtaken with such faults. A very old pastor was once asked when that desire goes away? He responded, "I will let you know when it does." I was in the counseling room with a young pastor who was questioning if he should remain in the ministry. He had a sensitive conscience and was severely battered by the constant temptation of women in immodest apparel. He sought to take his thoughts captive to the obedience of Christ on a constant basis.

The Christian needs to be aware of places, circumstances, and those people that will throw fuel on the fire of lust. If a courtship is desired, it should be done in the purview of the covenant family. It is ridiculous to think that you can properly get to know someone by going on a series of superficial "dates". Anyone can put on an act and look good for a time when apart from their family and the family of God. A new wardrobe, some nice cologne or perfume, and a put-on smile can do wonders for impressions! You can tell a lot about someone by looking at how they treat their mother and respect their father. Young emotions will be held in check when mom and dad are near.

I love to drive fast, and I fight a youthful lust to put the pedal-to-the-metal. Those lusts are more easily controlled when I am in the presence of a police car! Accountability is the Lord's means to help His children with resisting lusts. It is not good for a man or woman to be alone, with a computer or with one another. These emotions are like a car with no brakes going down hill!

Day 29

THE BORN-AGAIN MARLBORO MAN

"Help, LORD; for the godly man ceaseth;
for the faithful fail from among the
children of men." —Psalm 12:1

Do you remember the Marlboro man? You know, the one on the billboard with the rugged good looks sitting high atop a majestic steed in his well-worn blue jeans, boots, and leather chaps. He squints out at us from under the brim of that iconic white cowboy hat, unshaven, with a look that exudes "coolness". But wait, what's that hanging out of his mouth? Well it's his cigarette, of course. The whole purpose of this long-running advertising campaign has been to portray the mark of a real man as smoking a bold cigarette!

It's sad that while nobody today can feign ignorance to the fact that smoking causes cancer, or ignore the lesser side-effects of stained teeth, offensive smoker's breath, and the stink that clings to one's clothes, polluting both car and home, there are still millions who are addicted to the image of the Marlboro man!

These poor dupes have bought into a lie that costs them hundreds of dollars a month at five dollars a pack, thousands in medical bills, years off their life, and perhaps their last healthy breath! The idol-craving pop-culture of the day has also set up its false image of a "real" man. Have you ever seen a female teenager decorate her wall with a poster of Billy Graham sporting his black Bible and garbed in his conservative suit and tie? These are not men who are respected today, instead there's a craving for men that live life in the fast lane of immorality. It's easy for a dead fish to swim downstream. Any man can live an ungodly life. It is not hard to use filthy language, drink beer and sleep around. Just about anyone can get a tattoo, workout and ride a motorcycle.

The Bible paints a completely different picture of what it means to be a real man. The Superman of the Bible is Jesus Christ. He is the Hero for all mankind to imitate. He is the ultimate picture of what a man should be. He was first and foremost god-glorifying. He knew no sin and sought to live a holy life according to the Scriptures. A real man is one who pursues holiness in his heart and life. There will be visible fruits of his daily mortification of the deeds of the flesh.

A real man will evidence humility when he makes mistakes. He will show forth repentance, and seek forgiveness. He will be a praying man. He will pray at church, in private and with his family. He will be a man of the Bible. He will not have a self-righteous attitude towards others.

He will lead his family in worship, both in the home and in the church. He will wash his wife with the water of the word by reading and explaining biblical principles. He will cherish the wife of his youth with time and attention.

Children, if and when he has them, are a top-priority for the real man. He will train up his children by virtue of the Bible's teachings and by his godly example. He will spend time with his children and take joy in the simple things that they like to do. He will be approachable and able to communicate effectively. A real man can roll around on the floor and have fun but is not a push-over when discipline is necessary. He can compassionately listen and weep as hurts are shared. He is not unable to hug and kiss his family with sincere affection. In fact he understands that an austere, stoic demeanor is not what defines a real man. He will not seek to get out of his responsibilities. He swears to his own hurt and does whatever is necessary to provide for his family.

The real man may have his hobbies and personal pursuits, but never at the expense of his God or his family. He is faithful at work, in the home and in the church. He supports the public gatherings of the brethren. He has a high esteem for his Elders. He gladly submits himself and his family under the authority of his Pastor. He has a teachable spirit coupled with a humble desire to grow into a further image of Christ. That is the real man!

Picture this on the billboards of America's highways— The Marlboro man has been saved and is radically changed! The eyes of young men look up to a man carrying his Bible as he leads his family into the local church to participate in vibrant worship and receive instruction and encouragement to live a holy life!

Day 30

SUCCESSFUL LIVING

**"For we shall all stand before the judgment
seat of Christ." —Romans 14:10**

Have you heard the common misconception that
"He who dies with the most toys wins?" It's a misnomer
that continues to permeate the hearts of lost people.
There seems to be an insatiable appetite for more and
more "stuff". Rockefeller was once asked, "How much is
enough?" His reply was classic of the lust-monster that
lurks within the heart of depravity, "A little more than
what you have." We need to debunk the myth that we can
take anything with us when we make our departure from
this world. We leave the same way we came in. No need
to bury grandma with her jewelry. Although life is not a
game, there are rules and rewards for those who run its
race and finish well.

Our text tells us that we shall all stand before the judgment seat of Christ. The entire life of each soul will be
examined according to the Law of the Lord. This is an
individual, one-at-a-time happening, as opposed to a

corporate federalism. Each of us will have our day in the court of Heaven. Every idle word and all of our works, whether good or bad, will be brought before the feet of Christ for examination.

Jesus Christ will not only judge Christians. He is the only judge for all of mankind. You must understand that every knee will bow to Him and confess their acknowledgment that He is who He has revealed Himself to be. It is interesting to note that even Hell will be filled with those who've had a personal experience of Christ! They will have all personally stood before Him, bowed their knee to Him, and confessed Him to be Lord! None of the toys people strive their whole lives long to accumulate will be allowed in the courtroom.

As the Creator of the whole world Jesus has the right to Judge. He is the one that created man. He is the one that created us Christians. He has given us all things that pertain to life and godliness. He has equipped us for the work of the ministry. As general revelation leaves all of mankind without an excuse to acknowledge the existence and glory of God, the special revelation of the inward work of the Holy Ghost leaves the believer without an excuse to have been obedient and fruitful. The first step to living successfully is having eternity in view. The ancient Orientals had a custom when inaugurating a new leader. They would ceremoniously place three blocks of marble before him from which to choose. Whichever one he chose was made into his own tombstone and would serve as a reminder to him of his mortality.

In the Bible, life is likened to a vapor. As slow as it may seem at times, it goes by very fast. It is extremely frail and unpredictable. People are shaken at night and pass away. Death is no respecter of age, sex, or ethnicity. Death has been appointed unto all men. After death is the judgment. One can deny the existence of the sun, but it will still shine. There is a prize for those who live successfully in the eyes of Christ. He will not be counting the amount of toys that we've acquired.

The vanity of bigger barns, houses and bank accounts, will be evidence used against those who love their "stuff" more than godliness; but it will be a glorious day for those who love Jesus and desire to be saved from their sins. He will wash away all tears and carry each of His dear children safely to His heavenly kingdom of grace and truth. Dear reader, rather than earthly treasure, make the goal of your life to receive the Lord's commendation, "Well done thou good and faithful servant."

About The Author

Chris Hatton was born and raised on eastern Long Island, NY. In 1989, at the age of nineteen, he was converted through the witness of his English professor Dr. Tom Bennett while attending Daytona State College. Chris married his high school sweetheart Denise that same year and was soon faced with the tragic death of his adopted brother and best friend. It was the suicide of his nineteen year old brother Jimmy that gave Chris a deep burden to share the good news of hope In Christ. This passion was soon recognized by his local church and Chris was licensed in 1992 and ordained in 1994 to preach the Gospel. He was on the streets seeking to serve and share until his elders sent him to formal study. Chris earned a B.R.E., M.Div, and D.Min, from Davis Bible College, Mid-America Baptist Theological Seminary, and South Atlantic Theological Seminary, respectively. While studying Chris led the university evangelistic teams to state prison ministry, children homes, nursing homes, street evangelism, and state college campus ministry.

Chris came to understand the ministerial priority of the local church as he was groomed in historical confessional christianity by some older 1689 Pastors. He served in several Association of Reformed Baptist Churches of America (ARBCA). He is currently on the pastoral staff at Grace Chapel in Sanford Florida (www.gracereformedchapel.org). Chris is also the founder and Pastoral Chair of the Reformation Society of Florida (www.AllianceNet.org) and the Spurgeon Fellowship of Florida (www.spurgeonfellowshipfl.com). Chris and His wife homeschool their children in central Florida and he can be contacted at faith92@juno.com.

THE MISSION OF GREAT CHRISTIAN BOOKS

The ministry of Great Christian Books was established to glorify The Lord Jesus Christ and to be used by Him to expand and edify the kingdom of God while we occupy and anticipate Christ's glorious return. Reformation Press will seek to accomplish this mission by publishing Gospel literature which is biblically faithful, relevant, and practically applicable to many of the serious spiritual needs of mankind upon the verge of a new millennium. To do so we will always seek to boldly incorporate the truths of Scripture, especially those which were largely articulated as a body of theology during The Protestant Reformation of the sixteenth century and ensuing years. We gladly join our voice in the proclamations of— Scripture Alone, Faith Alone, Grace Alone, Christ Alone, and God's Glory Alone!

Our ministry seeks the blessing of our God as we seek His face to both confirm and support our labors for Him. Our prayers for this work can be summarized by two verses from the Book of Psalms:

"...let the beauty of the LORD our God be upon us, And establish the work of our hands for us; Yes, establish the work of our hands." —Psalm 90:17

"Not unto us, O LORD, not unto us, but to your name give glory." —Psalm 115:1

Great Christian Books appreciates the financial support of anyone who shares our burden and vision for publishing literature which combines sound Bible doctrine and practical exhortation in an age when too few so-called "Christian" publications do the same. We thank you in advance for any assistance you can give us in our labors to fulfill this important mission. May God bless you.

For a catalog of other great
Christian books including
additional titles by
Chris Hatton contact us in
any of the following ways:

write us at:
Reformation Press
160 37th Street
Lindenhurst, NY 11757

call us at:
631. 956. 0998

find us online:
www.greatchristianbooks.com

email us at:
mail@greatchristianbooks.com

www.ingramcontent.com/pod-product-compliance
Lightning Source LLC
Chambersburg PA
CBHW070525030426
42337CB00016B/2115